YOUR KNOWLEDGE HAS VALUE

AF136301

- We will publish your bachelor's and
  master's thesis, essays and papers

- Your own eBook and book -
  sold worldwide in all relevant shops

- Earn money with each sale

Upload your text at www.GRIN.com
and publish for free

Circumstances under which a Partnership Firm is equivalent to a Private Limited Company

Datius Didace

Bibliographic information published by the German National Library:

The German National Library lists this publication in the National Bibliography; detailed bibliographic data are available on the Internet at http://dnb.dnb.de.

ISBN: 9783346663306
This book is also available as an ebook.

© GRIN Publishing GmbH
Nymphenburger Straße 86
80636 München

All rights reserved

Print and binding: Books on Demand GmbH, Norderstedt, Germany
Printed on acid-free paper from responsible sources.

The present work has been carefully prepared. Nevertheless, authors and publishers do not incur liability for the correctness of information, notes, links and advice as well as any printing errors.

GRIN web shop: https://www.grin.com/document/1239513

CIRCUMSTANCES UNDER WHICH PARTNERSHIP FIRM IS EQUIVALENT TO THE PRIVATE LIMITED COMPANY

BY;

DATIUS

DIDACE

RUBANZA-LWABUGIRWA

1.0 INTRODUCTION.

The law related to business association covers different aspects such as sole traders, partnership as well as company law, whereby each of it is governed by law as well as by practice, For example partnership is governed by The Contract Act[1] and Company law is governed by The Company Act[2]. The focus of this work is to discuss on whether in the modern business association a partnership firm is equivalent to the private limited company. The work is divided in several parties such as introduction, main body and conclusion. In introduction the question will be introduced and the related term will be defined therein, the main body will cover the whole discussion of the work, then we shall make conclusion of this work. Different law such as statutes and case law will be applied to make the work meaningful as personal examples will be used to clarify some points as discussed herebelow;

1.1 MEANING OF TERMS

As for the purpose of this work the following terms have been defined here as follows,

COMPANY

There is no precise legal definition of a company. This is to historical reasons which are too wide to be narrated. Suffice it to say that the word "company" is

---

[1] Cap 345 R.E 2019
[2] Act No 12 of 2002

a product of mercantile rather than legal ingenuity and was used in England long before what is now called "Company law" came into existence[3]

The word **"Company"** is an amalgamation of the Latin word **"com"** meaning **"with or together** and **"pains"** meaning **"bread".** Originally, it referred to the group of person who took their meals together. Hence a company is nothing but
a group of people who have come together or who have contributed money for some common purpose and who have incorporated themselves into a legal entity.

According to **Oxford Concise Law Dictionary[4]**, a company is an association of persons formed for the purpose of some business or undertaking carried on in a companies' name. **Section 2 of the Companies Act[5]** provides that, a company means a company formed and registered under the Act. In the
case of **SMITH V. ANDERSON[6]** it was stated that, accompany is an association of individuals formed for some common purpose. \

Consequently, **Lord Palmer** in the case of **SOLOMON vs. SOLOMON AND COMPANY LTD[7]** to mean *"a legal person or a legal entity separate from, and capable of surviving beyond the lives of, its members capable of*
rights and duties of its own, and endowed with the potential perpetual succession."

---

[3] J.J Ogola, Company Law, 1st edition pg1
[4] See at pg 79
[5] Act no 12 Of 2002
[6] (1880) 15 Ch. D 247
[7] [1895-99] ALL ER Rep 33:66

In a nutshell, the defining characteristics of a company are such as, **"separate entity"**; **"limited liability"**; **"perpetual succession"** having separate property, transferability of shares, capacity to sue or being sued as well as separate management. These characteristics give a company the ability to be recognized

in law, under the eyes of principle referred to as the veil of incorporation that is the fictional veil (and not wall between the company and its members.

PARTNERSHIP

Partnership has been defined under **section 190(1)** of the **Contract Act**[8] as is the relationship which subsists between persons carrying on business in

common as defined with a view of profit. **Kapoor** defines partnership as the relationship between persons who have agreed to share the profits of a business carried on by all or any of them acting for all[9]. The term **Partnership firm** therefore, refers to persons who have entered into partnership with one another in a collective firm and the name under which their business is carried on[10]. It is the business that established between persons who have agreed to share the profits of the business carried on by all or any of the member of the business[11].

Hence, the right to form partnerships is a constitutional right which is provided for by the provisions of Article 20(1)[12]. With partnerships there must be persons who are obliged to conduct themselves. These are called partners and when they are collective, they are called a firm. Nevertheless, partners in a social relation should be differentiated from partners in business. This is because partners in a business are individual persons formed into a

---

[8] Cap 345 R E 2019

[9] Kapoor N,D(2006) Element of Mercantile Law including Company Law and Industrial Law,28th Edn ,Sultan Chand & Sons Publishers ,New Delhi.

[10] See section 190(2) of the Contract Act Cap 345 R E 2019

[11] Keenan D. (1986) Mercantile Law,6th Edn, Pitman Publishing Limited, London, pg 220.

[12] The Constitution of the United Republic of Tanzania, 1977 as amended from time to time

partnership with the aim of sharing the profits of a business. On the other hand, the former only meet on no common ground and with no need of obtaining any profit from any business.

- **Types of Partnerships**

There are many types of partnerships but which can be grouped as follows: general and special partnerships, trading and non- trading partnerships. A general partnership is created for the general conduct of a particular kind of business, such as a hardware business or a manufacturing business. On the other hand, a special partnership is formed for a single transaction, such as the purchase and resale of a certain building. Moreover, trading partnerships are organized for the purpose of buying and selling, such as a firm engaged in the retail grocery business. On the contrary, a non-trading partnership is one organized for a purpose other than engaging in commerce, such as the practice of law or medicine[13]. From there we get the classes of partners which include; general partners, sleeping or dormant partners, limited and quasi partners or partners by holding out (nominal partners)[14].

PRIVATE COMPANY

Private Company has been define under company Act as to mean, a company which by its articles restricts the right to transfer its shares and limits the number of its member to fifty, not including persons who are in the employment of the company and person who; having been formerly in the employment of the company, were while in that employment, and have continued after the determination of that employment to be member of company and prohibits any invitation to the public to subscribe for any shares

---

[13] Anderson Ronald A., et al, (1987), Business Law, Revised Edition, South- Western Publishing Co., Ohio, p. 777

[14] Ibid. p.778

or debentures of the company.[15] The **private company** is forbidden to go to the public for funds and in return enjoys the benefit of having to observe fewer formalities before it can start business[16].

A private limited company is a type of privately held small business entity which limits owner liability to their shares, limits the number of shareholders to

50, and restricts shareholders from publicly trading shares. Features of the private limited company includes that it is a separate legal entity separate from

its owners and shareholders, it has perpetual succession in the sense that its life or continuity is not affected by the life of its members, it has restriction on transferability of shares as well as the limitation of member's liability.

This is normally what American call a close corporation. A private company (sometimes referred as to quasi-partnership company) in the nature of

partnership of persons with mutual confidence in each other and its article place positive restrictions on absolute transfer of shares as per section 27(1) (a) of the **Companies Act**[17]. The private company has the following characteristics:

> *(a) Restricted membership. Section 27(1) (b) of the Companies Act[18] limits the number of its members to fifty. In determining this number of fifty, employee-members and ex-employee members are not to be considered.*
>
> *(b) Restrict the rights of members to transfer its shares as per section 27(1) (a) of the Companies Act.[19]*
>
> *(c) Prohibits any invitation to the public to subscribe to any shares in or the debentures of the company as per section 27(1) (c) of the Companies*

---

[15] See section 27 (1)(a)(b)(c) of the company Act No 12 of 2002
[16] Chorley M,A and Giles O,C.(1972)Mercantile Law,16th Edition, Pitman Publishing,g166.
[17] Ibid
[18] No. 12 of 2002
[19] Op. cit

Act[20]. The Act creates an offence for a private company which is not a private company limited by guarantee and not having share capital to offer to the public (whether for cash or otherwise) any share in or debenture of a company.

MEANING OF PUBLIC COMPANY:

Public Company means a company, which is not a private company. A Public Company usually has got the following characteristics:

(a) *The general public is allowed to subscribe for membership on fulfilling of few general conditions. The minimum number of member is seven.*

(b) *It can not commence business unless it obtains certificate of commencement of business.*

(c) *The memorandum of public company shall state that it is a public company.*

(d) *Transfer of shares is free.*

Under the Companies Act a Public Company is the company limited by shares or guarantee and having a share capital, being a company the memorandum of which states that it is to be a public company.

1.2 GENERAL CHARACTERISTICS OF A COMPANY:

A company as an entity has a several distinct features which together make it a unique organization. The following are the defining characteristics of a company:

Independent corporate existence: this is one of the essential features of a company. The company is a juristic person. It ha separate legal entity. The company is association of persons formed for that purpose of some business or undertaking carried on the name of association. But at the same time it has its own independent corporate existence, which is called **corporate personality**. It is also known as **"Rule of SOLOMON vs. SOLOMON"**. It is

---

formed with the members, and at the same time it is independent of its members. It is corporate aggregate. It functions as a corporate sole. The company is at law a different person altogether from its members.

This is also called as *"The veil of Corporation"*. The theory of the corporate entity is indeed, the basic principle on which the whole law of corporation. The theory which explains about the Corporate Personality is known as **Organic Theory**.

Limited liability: is also the feature of the company. This means the liability of the member is limited to the extent of his shares only. In a partnership firm, the liability is liable to the complete extent, even personality also. When the company had been registered, it follows from the fact that a corporation is a separate person that its members are not as such liable for its debts. Hence in absence of express provision to the contrary the member will be completely free from any personal liability. This, is in fact, the position as regards municipal and ecclesiastical corporations and rapidly decreasing number of public corporations, and may be so as regards statutory and chartered companies, the member of which will be under personal liability only if, and to the extent that, the statutes or charter provides.[21]

Perpetual succession: is another feature of the company. One of the obvious advantage of artificial person is that is not susceptible to "the thousand natural shocks that flesh is heir to." It can not incapacitate by illness, mental or physical, and it has not (or need not have) an allotted span of life. This is not to say that the death or incapacity of its human

---

[21] Davis, L.P, Gower's the Principle of Modern Company Law.

members may not cause the company considerable embarrassment; obvious it will if all the directors die or imprisoned or if there are too few surviving members to hold a valid meeting, or if the bulk of the members or directors become enemy aliens.[22] The death of a member leaves the company unmoved; members may come and go but the company can go on for ever. During the 1939- 1945 War all members of one private company, while in general meeting, were killed by a bomb. But the company survived; not even the hydrogen bomb could have destroyed it.[23]

Separate property: is one of the essential features of a company. Among the obvious advantage of corporate personality is that it enables the property of the association to be more clearly distinguished from that of its members. In an incorporated society, the property of the association is the joint property of the members.[24]In that regards therefore, the company is a juristic person. It has its own legal entity. It has its own property. It is liable for its own debts. It is independent to the members. The members' liability limited to the extent of their shares only. In the case of **MACAURA vs. NORTHERN ASSURANCE Co. LTD**[25], Walton, J, explained that: ***"the property of the company is not the property of the shareholders. It is the property of the company."***

Capacity to sue and be sued: is also the essential feature of a company. The company comes into existence from the date on which the certificate of incorporation is granted. This certificate brings the company into existence as a legal person. It can sue and be sued in its own name. In the words of **Bankes, L.J**, in **BANGUE INTERNATIONALE DE COMMERCE**

---

[22] Daimler Co vs. Continental Tyre and Rubber Company [1916] 2 A.C 307, H.L.
[23] Davis, L.P, Gower's the Principle of Modern Company Law.
[24] Ibid
[25] (1925) A.C 619

DE PETROGRAD vs. GOANKASSAOW[26], "the party seeking to maintain the action is in the eye of he law no party at all but a mere name only, with no legal existence...A non-existence person can not sue, and once the court is made aware that the plaintiff is non-existence, and therefore incapable of maintaining the action, it cannot allow the action to proceed.

Separate management: also constitute the essential feature of a company. A company is administered and managed by its managerial personnel i.e. the Board of Directors. The shareholders are simply the holders of the shares in the company and need not be necessarily the managers of the company.

Transferable shares: is an important feature of a company: share of a public company can easily be transferable as compared with a private company. Section 74 of the **Companies Act**[27] provides that, *"the shares or other interest of any member in a company shall be movable property transferable in a manner provided by the articles of the company."* In this regards therefore, shares in a public company are freely transferable, subject to certain conditions, such that no shareholder is permanently or necessarily wedded to a company. When a member transfers his shares his shares to another person, the transferee steps into the shoes of the transferor and acquires all rights of the transferor in respect of those shares. Though the provision of **section 27(1) (a)** of the **Companies Act**[28]restrict the transfer of the private company subject to certain limitations, this still remain to be an essential feature of a company. The

---

[26] (1923) 2. K.B 682 at 688
[27] No. 12 of 2002
[28] No. 12 of 2002

section provides that, *"the private company means a company which by its articles restricts the right to transfer its shares."*

According to section 28 of the **Companies Act**[29] states that if a private company alters its articles such that they no longer include the provisions required for private company as per section 27 of the Act, the company shall on the date of the alteration, cease to be a private company and shall amend its memorandum to state that it is a public company. The company should within 14 days send notification to the registrar who shall issue a certificate to the effect that the company is the public company.

2.0 FORMATION OF PARTNERSHIP FIRM AND PRIVATE LIMITED COMPANY

Before tracing whether in modern business association a partnership firm is equivalent to the private limited company it is better first to understand how this two business association are be formed;

The Partnership Firm. This type of business association is governed by Contract Act[30] especially under part xi of the Act. It can be formed when the following has been established;

Association of two or more persons, This means that to constitute a partnership firm there must be at least two or more

---

[29] Ibid
[30] Ibid, fn no 1

persons with common intention of conducting business for the profit as the definition of partnership is concern.

Agreement (Partnership deed), Partnership firm is the result of agreement between members as explained under **section 191(1)**[31] that "the relationship of partnership arises from contract and not from status." Its formation therefore depends up on agreement of the firm members who consented with legal object and lawful consideration. The agreement can be oral or written and in it, all agreement must be shown.

The business to be carried out, this means that for the partnership firm to be established there must be a specific business to be conducted or carried out, As according to **section 190(1)** for the partnership to stand, there must be a business to be carried on for the common intention of getting profit. The above factors makes the formation of partnership firm. That if the above factors are present the partnership firm is formed.

The Private Limited Company. This type of business association is governed by The Law of Company Act,[32]The formation of Private limited company happen when two or more persons agree to join together to form a company. Some time it originates from the partnership. That once a partnership firm extend in its capital and membership to fifty, a partnership expand and became private limited company.

---

[31] Cap 345 R E 2019
[32] Act No 13 of 2002.

2.1 DIFFERENCE BETWEEN PARTNERSHIP AND PRIVATE LIMITED COMPANY:

2.1.1 Formation

The formation of the partnership firm is quite different to that of private limited company. The difference in formation exists under various aspects including the **law governing its formation**. Whereas, formation of private limited company is as provided under the Chapter 1 of Part II of the **Company Act**[33] while the partnership formation is as provided under the **Law of Contract Act.**[34] Moreover, difference under formation aspect exist in the **minimum number of members** required for the formation. Such that under partnership the minimum number of members required when initiating a partnership firm is **two members** differently from the Private Company Limited. Whereas previously under section 3[35] it required two members as minimum number, however, following the amendments done under the **Written Law Amendment Act No. 2 of 2012**[36] provides that private company can be formed by **one member**. All in all, a partnership does not acquire a legal entity even if it is registered under the existing law[37]. In the case of **Shain Investment Co., Inc. vs. Cohen**[38], it was held that a partnership is a voluntary association and exists because the parties agree to be in partnership. The implication here is that if there is no agreement then there is no partnership.

---

[33] Act No. 12 of 2002
[34] [Cap 345 R.E 2019]
[35] Company Act, Act No. 12 of 2002
[36] Section 18 of the Act
[37] Saharay, H.K. (2008), Company Law, 5th Ed., Universal Law Publishing Company,.
[38] 15 Mass App 4,443 NE2d 126 (1982).

2.1.2 Legal entity

Unlike the private limited company, a **partnership has no separate legal status** apart from its partners, as the partners are individually known as a partner and collectively known as firm. For instance, Section 202[39]provides that partners are bound by acts on behalf of firm unlike the Private company which is a separate legal entity.

A private limited company is a legal or artificial person having the separate identity, common seal and perpetual succession which is formed and governed by a law. A **company as a separate legal entity** has the ability of owning property, incurring debt and borrowing money, having a bank account, employing people, entering into contracts and suing and being sued separately from its members. As it was provided by Lord Macnaghten in the case of *Salomon v Salomon*[40]

"The company is at law a different person altogether from the subscribers to the memorandum, and though it may be that after incorporation the business is precisely the same as it was before, and the same persons are managers, and the same hands receive the profits, the company is not in law the agent of the subscribers or trustee of them. Nor are subscribers liable, in any shape or form except to the extent and in a manner provided by the Act"[41]

One among of the powers that a private company is entitled as a legal entity is the **capacity to sue and be sued under its own name**. This was similarly reiterated in the case of *Anthon Bronkhorst v. The Deposit Insurance*

---

[39] Law of Contract Act [Cap 345 R.E 2019]
[40] (1897) A.C 22
[41] Lubengo, H. & Laurent, J. Lecture Notes On Essentials Of Corporate Law. P. 3

Board (The Liquidator of FBME Bank Ltd (Under Liquidation)[42] where the court in determining if the FBME Bank had the locus standi stated that: the respondent being a Lebanese private limited company has the right to sue on its own capacity or being sued on his own name.

2.1.3 Limited liability

In the Partnership Firm, a **liability of the partners is unlimited** unlike under the Private Limited Company. Liability is limited to the extent of shares held by every member. The liability of the members of the private limited company is limited to contribution to the assets of the company up to the face value of **shares or guarantees** held by them. **Section 3(2)**[43] provides for the limited liability of the members of company to include company limited by shares, company limited by guarantees, company limited by both shares and guarantees and the company with unlimited liability. In a company limited by shares the liability of members is limited to the unpaid value of shares. In a company limited by guarantee, the liability of a member is limited to such amount, as the members may undertake to contribute to the assets of a company, in the events of its being wound up.[44]

The limited liability is of the importance that, it prevents its owners from being held personally responsible for the debts of the company. If the company goes bankrupt or is sued, the personal assets of its owner/investors cannot be

---

[42] Misc. Civil Application No.135 of 2020
[43] Company Act, Act No. 12 of 2002
[44] Lubengo, H. & Laurent, J. Lecture Notes On Essentials Of Corporate Law. P.4

pursued[45]. Rather the responsibility of the company member lies only on the number of shares or guarantee he/she owns.

2.1.4 Registration

Although both the partnership and the private limited company are registered at BRELA[46], the registration of the partnership firm is different to that of a Private Limited Company. Whereas registration of the private company is as provided and governed under the **Company Act**[47] while a business entity in a form of sole proprietorship or partnership must be registered under the **Business Names Registration Act**.

Moreover, under registration another difference lies in the necessary documents required. Such that, unlike the partnership registration, in registering a private company **memorandum and articles of association** is required as one among the important documents as well as the **certificate of incorporation.** Memorandum of association is a very important document in registration of the private limited company as it acts a s a constitution of the company and consists all the necessary information of the company.

2.1.5 Perpetual Succession

Unlike a partnership firm, a company has a perpetual succession. Meaning that a company does not die or cease to exist unless it is specifically wound up or the task for which it was formed has been completed. Membership of a company may keep on changing from time to time but that does not affect life

---

[45] Limited liability definition, retrieved from https://www.investopedia.com/terms/l/limitedliability.asp as accessed on 09/05/2022 at 11:49 AM
[46] Business Registration and Licensing Authority
[47] Act No. 12 of 2002

of the company[48]. Death or insolvency of members does not affect the existence of the company. A company is a creature of the law so its existence and non-existence is only determined and defined by the law. Unlike the partnership firm where on the death of any partner, the partnership is dissolved unless there is provision to the contrary[49]

2.1.6 Separate property

Unlike the partnership firm, the private limited company has a right to own its own properties separate from the properties of the individuals[50]. Under the Private limited company the property belongs to the company and not to its members while in partnership Property of the firm belongs to the partners and they are collectively entitled to it. A company is a distinct legal entity. The company's property is its own. A member cannot claim to be owner of the company's property during the existence of the company.[51]

2.1.7 Manners of dissolution

Dissolution of a company or a partnership firm is the situation where the company or the partnership firm existence is put to an end. Manners of dissolution of a private limited company differs to that of the partnership firm. Whereas, a partnership firm can be dissolved in two ways including the **judicial and the extrajudicial** by any one or all of the partners as provided under **Sections 212 and 215**[52] consecutively. On the other hand, a private

---

[48] Binamungu, C.S.M.,(2000), Business Law Students Manual, National Board of Accountants and Auditors, Dar es salaam.
[49] Anderson Ronald A., et al, (1987), **Business Law**, Revised Edition, South- Western Publishing Co., Ohio
[50] Kapoor, N.D, (2008), **Elements of Mercantile Law**, 29th Ed. Sultan Chand & Sons Educational Publishers, New Delhi.
[51] Lubengo, H. & Laurent, J. Lecture Notes On Essentials Of Corporate Law. P. 3
[52] Law of Contract Act [Cap 345 R.E 2019]

limited company cannot be wound up by any one or all of the members of the company. Meaning that dissolution of a private company can only be done by a **judicial process** only. This is because private company is a creature of a statute hence its dissolution must be done by a judicial process. The

dissolution of a company by the judicial process is as provided under **Section**

329[53] where the company is dissolved by the order of the court upon application.

2.2 CIRCUMSTANCES UNDER WHICH PARTNERSHIP FIRM IS EQUIVALENT TO THE PRIVATE LIMITED COMPANY:

With the growing trend of business transaction in the modern business as well the economy has affected the business association of today to the effect that in some circumstance the Partnership firm becomes as similar as private limited company in the following areas;

2.2.1 Number of Membership

These two types of business association have similarity in term of minimum number of membership, fore instance in order to have a partnership firm members must at least be more than one as the definition suggest, The same to private limited company membership of the company must be more than one persons as stipulated under **section 3(1)** of the Act which states as *'Any two or more persons, associated for any lawful purpose may, by subscribing their name to a memorandum of association and otherwise complying with requirement of this Act in respect of registration, form an incorporated company, with or without limited*

---

[53] Company Act, Act No. 12 of 2002

liability[54]".Also **section 27(2) of the Act** provides that *'where two or more persons hold one or more shares in a company jointly, they shall, for the purpose of this section, be treated as a single member'[55]*. Therefore this shows that both partnership firm and private limited company has similar minimum member of the business association.

2.2.2 Objectives

The modern partnership firm is equivalent to private limited company in terms of objectives where by both business association aiming at conducting business for profits. That means in partnership firm members aiming at sharing profits or losses equally or in proportion of their capital as stated in their partnership deed, **section 191(2)(a)(b) and (c) of the Contract Act[56]**,it provides for the rules in relation to the object of the firm. This is similar to private limited company that its objective is to obtain profits as **section 3(2)(a) and (b) of company Act(supra)** suggest.

2.2.3 Registration

This means that the partnership firm and private liability company are equal in term of registration, that both are to be registered

2.2.4 Transferable shares

The Transferable shares in both type of business transferability of share are limited, whereby in partnership firm transfer of shares are restricted and none of a member of partnership is allowed to transfer his share. Likewise in private

---

[54] See section 3(1) of Act No 12 of 2002
[55] Ibid,fn 12,section 27(2)
[56] Cap 345 R E 2019

limited company transferability of share are limited and members are restricted to transfer its shares as **section 27(1) (c) of company** Act directs.

2.2.5 Deed of Operation

The partnership firm is equivalent to the private limited company in terms of deed of operation whereby in partnership firm the firm must operate through a

deed of agreement known as *Articles of partnership deed or partnership agreement.*

This is similar to private limited company where the company must have

memorandum of association which in both act as a constitution of the business association. The partnership deed and memorandum of association are document of great importance to the firm as well as company respectively because they contain with fundamental conditions upon which the firm and company are allowed to perform its duty in day to day[57].

The partnership firm in modern business is equivalent to the private limited company because both are made up with the **attitude of secrecy of providing information on financial statement.** That in partnership firm only members of the firm are allowed to trace cash book and other financial information of the firm, this is likewise in private limited company whereby the whole activities of the company on cash matters are allowed to be viewed with only members of the company. This then makes the two business association to have similar character that makes them to be known as equal.

---

[57] Ibid,fn 4, pg 67

2.3 CIRCUMSTANCE UNDER WHICH PARTNERSHIP FIRM IS NOT EQUIVALENT TO THE PRIVATE LIMITED COMPANY:

Partnership is the relationship between persons who have agreed to share the profits of a business carried on by all or any of them acting for all. Person who have entered into partnership with one another are called individually partners and collectively a firm,[58]and that form a partnership firm which formed as a result two or more persons joined together. The development of this partnership therefore may lead to a private limited company. Therefore partnership firm in some circumstance is not equivalent to private company due to;

2.3.1 Law regulating

That a partnership firm is been regulated by the **Law of Contract Act cap 345 Revised Edition 2019**, it is therefore arose as contract and not from status,[59]While Private limited company is regulated by the company Act, **Act No 12 of 2002**, especially under section 3(1) and section 27 Of the Act. Therefore the modern business partnership firm under such circumstance is not equivalent to private limited company.

2.3.2 Legal status

That in partnership firm, a firm is not a person in the eyes of law, it is made up by several persons who agreed to form a partnership, it therefore cannot sue and be sued as it was stated in the case of **Salomon v Salomon**[60] While a private limited company has legal personality distinct from that of its member,

---

[58] Section 190(1) and (2) of the Contract Act, Cap 345 R E 2019
[59] Section 191(1) Cap 345 R E 2019
[60] (1897) A C 22.

therefore it can sue and be sued, this can be possible only if the company is registered, if it has not be registered a private company can not sue, this was observed in the case of **Fort Hall Bakery supply v Federic Muigai Wangoe,**[61] where a suit was instituted by an unregistered firm of over twenty members, court held that such a company cannot be recognise as having legal personality that can sue or be sued simply has not yet registered.

2.3.3 Liability of members

in case of partnership firm members are severally and jointly to the creditor of the firm, a creditor obtaining judgement against the firm can proceed against and attach the private property of any of the partner in the firm, While in the private limited company liability of the members of the company is limited to the contribution of the assets of the company up on the face value of shares held by them,[62]A member is liable to pay only the uncalled money due on shares held by him when called upon to pay and nothing more. The importance of limited liability was expressed in the case of **Senkin v Pharmaceutical society of GB** where court held that limited liability is the offspring of a proved necessity that, men should be entitled to engage in commercial pursuit without involving the whole of their fortune in that particular pursuit in which they are engaged, This then makes partnership firm in modern business to be not equivalent to private limited company.

---

[61] (1957) E .A. 472
[62] Taken from Lubengo H and Laurent J,Lecture Notes on Essentials of Corporate Law(LAW 650) pg 2

2.3.4 Management of the business

This means that partnership firm and private limited are not equivalent in terms of management of the business whereby under partnership the firm is being managed by members that every member of the partnership firm may take party in its management unless partnership deed provide otherwise as **section 194(a) to (g) of the contract Act**[63] directs.. Whereby in private limited company the affairs of the company are managed by its directors or managing directors and its members have no right to take part in its management.

2.3.5 Authority of membership

Authority of membership each partner in partnership firm is agent of the partnership; he can make contracts and incur liabilities so long as he acts in the ordinary course of the firm's business. On the other hand a shareholder is not an agent of the company and has no such a power to bind the company by his act. Its power general as shareholder is limited to those allowed by the objective clause in its Memorandum of Association as stated in the **Baird's case** [64] in this case court held that a shareholder in a private company is not an agent of the company and his act can not bind the whole of the company.

2.3.6 Dissolution

There is a difference on partnership firm and private company in terms of dissolution, that in partnership firm unless a partnership is entered into for a fixed period, it may be dissolved by the death or insolvency of a partner. This

---

[63] Cap 345 R E 2019
[64] (1870) Ch. App 725

can be observed under section 212 to 215 of the Act[65], while a company has a perpetual succession, no person in any circumstance affecting a member such

as death, insolvency or unsound mind will affect its existence, it come to an end only when it is wound up according to the provisions of the Company Act

that established it.

2.3.6 Membership

There is a difference between partnership firm and private limited company in

term of membership, whereby in partnership firm membership limits is fifteen while in private limited company the limits of its membership is fifty as Act number 12 of 2002 directs.

3.0 CONCLUSSION

The law relating to partnership in Tanzania has provided basic rules which govern the relationship between members, however due to the movement of business today some time partnership firm became equivalent to the private limited company especially when the partnership firm extend to its capacity in term of capital as well as membership. This work herein above discussed whether partnership firm is equivalent to private limited company in the modern business association, the work traced how both business association are been formed as well as circumstance under which they are equivalent and circumstances under which they are not equivalent.

---

[65] Cap 345 R. E 2019

REFERENCE

LIST OF STATUTES

The Constitution of the United Republic of Tanzania, 1977

Law of Contract Act [Cap 345 R.E 2019]

Company Act, Act No. 12 of 2002

LIST OF CASES

Salomon v Salomon (1897) A.C 22

Anthon Bronkhorst v. The Deposit Insurance Board (The Liquidator of FBME Bank Ltd (Under Liquidation) Misc. Civil Application No.135 of 2020

Fort Hall Bakery supply v Federic Muigai Wangoe (1957), E.A472.

Senkin v Pharmaceutical society of GB (1921) 1CH392.

Shain Investment Co., Inc. vs. Cohen 15 Mass App 4,443 NE2d 126 (1982).

LIST OF BOOKS

Lubengo, H. & Laurent, J. Lecture Notes On Essentials Of Corporate Law. P. 3

Anderson Ronald A., et al, (1987), Business Law, Revised Edition, South- Western Publishing Co., Ohio,.

Binamungu, C.S.M.,(2000), Business Law Students Manual, National Board of Accountants and Auditors, Dar es salaam.

Kapoor, N.D, (2004), Company Law and Secretarial Practice, 12th Ed., Sultan Chand & Sons, Educational Publishers, New Delhi.

ONLINE SOURCES

Business association definition, Retrieved from https://www.lawinsider.com/

Limited   liability   definition,   retrieved   from
https://www.investopedia.com/terms/l/limitedliability

Partnership Definition, Retrieved from
https://www.investopedia.com/terms//partnership.asp#:~:text=A%20partnership%20is%20a
%20formal,business%20and%20share%20its%20profits.

Similarities between partnership and Private limited company, retrieved from
https://www.ehow.co.uk/info_8392925_similarities-between-partnership-limited-
company.html

What is private limited company? Retrieved from https://study.com/academy/lesson/what-is-
a-private-limited-company-definition-advantages-disadvantages.html

YOUR KNOWLEDGE HAS VALUE

- We will publish your bachelor's and
  master's thesis, essays and papers

- Your own eBook and book -
  sold worldwide in all relevant shops

- Earn money with each sale

Upload your text at www.GRIN.com
and publish for free